PLANNING, PROGRAMMING, BUDGETING, AND EXECUTION

IN COMPARATIVE ORGANIZATIONS

VOLUME 7

Executive Summary for
Additional Case
Studies

STEPHANIE YOUNG | **MEGAN MCKERNAN** | **ANDREW DOWSE** | **NICOLAS JOUAN**
THEODORA OGDEN | **AUSTIN WYATT** | **MATTIAS EKEN** | **LINDA SLAPAKOVA**
NAOKO AOKI | **RYAN CONSAUL** | **LAURINDA L. ROHN** | **FRANK G. KLOTZ** | **MICHAEL SIMPSON**
JADE YEUNG | **SARAH W. DENTON** | **YULIYA SHOKH** | **CLARA LE GARGASSON**
CHARLOTTE KLEBERG | **PHOEBE FELICIA PHAM** | **MADISON WILLIAMS** | **ERIK SILFVERSTEN**
JAMES BLACK | **TURNER RUGGI** | **MAXIME SOMMERFELD ANTONIOU**
RAPHAEL S. COHEN | **JOHN P. GODGES** | **HEIDI PETERS** | **LAUREN SKRABALA**

Prepared for the Commission on Planning, Programming, Budgeting, and Execution Reform

Approved for public release; distribution is unlimited

For more information on this publication, visit **www.rand.org/t/RRA2195**-7.

About RAND

The RAND Corporation is a research organization that develops solutions to public policy challenges to help make communities throughout the world safer and more secure, healthier and more prosperous. RAND is nonprofit, nonpartisan, and committed to the public interest. To learn more about RAND, visit www.rand.org.

Research Integrity

Our mission to help improve policy and decisionmaking through research and analysis is enabled through our core values of quality and objectivity and our unwavering commitment to the highest level of integrity and ethical behavior. To help ensure our research and analysis are rigorous, objective, and nonpartisan, we subject our research publications to a robust and exacting quality-assurance process; avoid both the appearance and reality of financial and other conflicts of interest through staff training, project screening, and a policy of mandatory disclosure; and pursue transparency in our research engagements through our commitment to the open publication of our research findings and recommendations, disclosure of the source of funding of published research, and policies to ensure intellectual independence. For more information, visit www.rand.org/about/principles.

RAND's publications do not necessarily reflect the opinions of its research clients and sponsors.

Published by the RAND Corporation, Santa Monica, Calif.
© 2024 RAND Corporation
RAND® is a registered trademark.

Library of Congress Cataloging-in-Publication Data is available for this publication.
ISBN: 978-1-9774-1309-3

Cover design by Peter Soriano; adimas/Adobe Stock images.

Limited Print and Electronic Distribution Rights

About This Report

The U.S. Department of Defense's (DoD's) Planning, Programming, Budgeting, and Execution (PPBE) process is a key enabler for DoD to fulfill its mission. But in light of a dynamic threat environment, increasingly capable adversaries, and rapid technological changes, there has been increasing concern that DoD's resource planning processes are too slow and inflexible to meet warfighter needs.[1] As a result, Congress mandated the formation of a legislative commission in Section 1004 of the National Defense Authorization Act for Fiscal Year 2022 to (1) examine the effectiveness of the PPBE process and adjacent DoD practices, particularly with respect to defense modernization; (2) consider potential alternatives to these processes and practices to maximize DoD's ability to respond in a timely manner to current and future threats; and (3) make legislative and policy recommendations to improve such processes and practices for the purposes of fielding the operational capabilities necessary to outpace near-peer competitors, providing data and analytical insight, and supporting an integrated budget that is aligned with strategic defense objectives.[2]

The Commission on PPBE Reform requested that the National Defense Research Institute provide an independent analysis of PPBE-like functions in selected countries and selected non-DoD federal agencies. The commission used insights from these analyses to derive lessons and convey recommendations to Congress on PPBE reform.

This executive summary distills key insights from a series of case studies of budgeting processes across seven comparative organizations, as detailed in the following two companion volumes:

- *Planning, Programming, Budgeting, and Execution in Comparative Organizations:* Vol. 5, *Additional Case Studies of Selected Allied and Partner Nations*
- *Planning, Programming, Budgeting, and Execution in Comparative Organizations:* Vol. 6, *Additional Case Studies of Selected Non-DoD Federal Agencies.*[3]

---

[1] See, for example, Section 809 Panel, *Report of the Advisory Panel on Streamlining and Codifying Acquisition Regulations*, Vol. 2 of 3, June 2018, pp. 12–13; Brendan W. McGarry, *DOD Planning, Programming, Budgeting, and Execution (PPBE): Overview and Selected Issues for Congress*, Congressional Research Service, R47178, July 11, 2022, p. 1; and William Greenwalt and Dan Patt, *Competing in Time: Ensuring Capability Advantage and Mission Success Through Adaptable Resource Allocation*, Hudson Institute, February 2021, pp. 9–10.

[2] Public Law 117-81, National Defense Authorization Act for Fiscal Year 2022, December 27, 2021.

[3] Stephanie Young, Megan McKernan, Andrew Dowse, Nicolas Jouan, Theodora Ogden, Austin Wyatt, Mattias Eken, Linda Slapakova, Naoko Aoki, Clara Le Gargasson, Charlotte Kleberg, Maxime Sommerfeld Antoniou, Phoebe Felicia Pham, Jade Yeung, Turner Ruggi, Erik Silfversten, James Black, Raphael S. Cohen, John P. Godges, Heidi Peters, and Lauren Skrabala, *Planning, Programming, Budgeting, and Execution in Comparative Organizations:* Vol. 5, *Additional Case Studies of Selected Allied and Partner Nations*, RAND Corporation, RR-A2195-5, 2024; Stephanie Young, Megan McKernan, Ryan Consaul, Laurinda L. Rohn, Frank G. Klotz, Michael Simpson, Sarah W. Denton, Yuliya Shokh, Madison Williams, Raphael S. Cohen,

In advance of the above volumes, the following four related volumes presented nine case studies of PPBE-like processes in selected countries and selected non-DoD federal agencies:

- *Planning, Programming, Budgeting, and Execution in Comparative Organizations:* Vol. 1, *Case Studies of China and Russia*
- *Planning, Programming, Budgeting, and Execution in Comparative Organizations:* Vol. 2, *Case Studies of Selected Allied and Partner Nations*
- *Planning, Programming, Budgeting, and Execution in Comparative Organizations:* Vol. 3, *Case Studies of Selected Non-DoD Federal Agencies*
- *Planning, Programming, Budgeting, and Execution in Comparative Organizations:* Vol. 4, *Executive Summary.*[4]

These reports should be of particular interest to stakeholders in DoD's PPBE processes and U.S. government officials who are involved in improving these processes.

The research reported here was completed in August 2023 and underwent security review with the sponsor and the Defense Office of Prepublication and Security Review before public release.

RAND National Security Research Division

This research was sponsored by the Commission on PPBE Reform and conducted within the Acquisition and Technology Policy Program of the RAND National Security Research Division (NSRD), which operates the National Defense Research Institute (NDRI), a federally funded research and development center sponsored by the Office of the Secretary of Defense,

John P. Godges, Heidi Peters, and Lauren Skrabala, *Planning, Programming, Budgeting, and Execution in Comparative Organizations:* Vol. 6, *Additional Case Studies of Selected Non-DoD Federal Agencies*, RAND Corporation, RR-A2195-6, 2024.

[4] Megan McKernan, Stephanie Young, Timothy R. Heath, Dara Massicot, Mark Stalczynski, Ivana Ke, Raphael S. Cohen, John P. Godges, Heidi Peters, and Lauren Skrabala, *Planning, Programming, Budgeting, and Execution in Comparative Organizations:* Vol. 1, *Case Studies of China and Russia*, RAND Corporation, RR-A2195-1, 2024; Megan McKernan, Stephanie Young, Andrew Dowse, James Black, Devon Hill, Benjamin J. Sacks, Austin Wyatt, Nicolas Jouan, Yuliya Shokh, Jade Yeung, Raphael S. Cohen, John P. Godges, Heidi Peters, and Lauren Skrabala, *Planning, Programming, Budgeting, and Execution in Comparative Organizations:* Vol. 2, *Case Studies of Selected Allied and Partner Nations*, RAND Corporation, RR-A2195-2, 2024; Megan McKernan, Stephanie Young, Ryan Consaul, Michael Simpson, Sarah W. Denton, Anthony Vassalo, William Shelton, Devon Hill, Raphael S. Cohen, John P. Godges, Heidi Peters, and Lauren Skrabala, *Planning, Programming, Budgeting, and Execution in Comparative Organizations:* Vol. 3, *Case Studies of Selected Non-DoD Federal Agencies*, RAND Corporation, RR-A2195-3, 2024; Megan McKernan, Stephanie Young, Timothy R. Heath, Dara Massicot, Andrew Dowse, Devon Hill, James Black, Ryan Consaul, Michael Simpson, Sarah W. Denton, Anthony Vassalo, Ivana Ke, Mark Stalczynski, Benjamin J. Sacks, Austin Wyatt, Jade Yeung, Nicolas Jouan, Yuliya Shokh, William Shelton, Raphael S. Cohen, John P. Godges, Heidi Peters, and Lauren Skrabala, *Planning, Programming, Budgeting, and Execution in Comparative Organizations:* Vol. 4, *Executive Summary*, RAND Corporation, RR-A2195-4, 2024.

the Joint Staff, the Unified Combatant Commands, the Navy, the Marine Corps, the defense agencies, and the defense intelligence enterprise.

For more information on the RAND Acquisition and Technology Policy (ATP) Program, see www.rand.org/nsrd/atp or contact the director (contact information is provided on the webpage).

Acknowledgments

We thank the members of the Commission on PPBE Reform—Robert Hale, Ellen Lord, Jonathan Burks, Susan Davis, Lisa Disbrow, Eric Fanning, Peter Levine, Jamie Morin, David Norquist, Diem Salmon, Jennifer Santos, Arun Seraphin, Raj Shah, and John Whitley—and staff for their dedication and deep expertise in shaping this work. We extend special gratitude to the commission chair, the Honorable Robert Hale; the vice chair, the Honorable Ellen Lord; executive director Lara Sayer; director of research Elizabeth Bieri; and the commission's senior researcher Kelle McCluskey for their guidance and support throughout this analysis. We would also like to thank the subject-matter experts on France, Germany, Japan, Singapore, Sweden, the U.S. Department of Veterans Affairs, and the National Nuclear Security Administration who provided us with valuable insights on these countries' and agencies' PPBE-like processes.

From NSRD, we thank Barry Pavel, vice president and director; Mike Spirtas, former associate director; Caitlin Lee, ATP director; and Aaron Frank, former acting ATP associate director, for their counsel and tireless support. We also thank our team of peer reviewers who offered helpful feedback on individual case studies and on cross-case takeaways. Finally, we would like to thank Maria Falvo and Saci Haslam for their administrative assistance during this effort. The work is much improved by virtue of their inputs, but any errors remain the responsibility of the authors alone.

Dedication

These volumes are dedicated to Irv Blickstein, whose decades of experience within the U.S. Navy's PPBE community deeply informed this work and whose intellectual leadership as a RAND colleague for more than 20 years greatly enhanced the quality of our independent analysis for DoD's most-pressing acquisition challenges. Irv's kindness, motivation, and ever-present mentoring will be sorely missed.

Summary

The Commission on Planning, Programming, Budgeting, and Execution (PPBE) Reform asked RAND to conduct case studies of the budgeting processes first across nine and then eventually across a total of 16 organizations: ten international defense organizations (including two near-peer competitors) and six other U.S. federal government agencies. The commission used insights from these analyses to derive lessons for the U.S. Department of Defense (DoD) and recommendations to Congress on PPBE reform.

Overarching Observations

A synthesis of key insights from the seven case studies presented in Volumes 5 and 6—and the applicability of those insights to DoD's PPBE System—led to the following overarching observations for the commission:

- A balance needs to be struck between enabling innovation and agility and ensuring the budget stability and predictability required for complex, long-term development efforts.
- Risk aversion in resource planning because of oversight, efficiency, and affordability considerations could be in conflict with efforts that enable innovation and agility.
- Beyond resource planning processes, military modernization requires a strong and broad-based societal foundation—with a trained workforce, an industrial capacity, innovation policies, national investments, and long-term planning and coordination of these inputs.
- DoD resource planning policies and decisions have implications for defense industrial base health and interdependent, co-development efforts with allies and partners.
- Continuing resolutions and other sources of budgetary uncertainty that impede DoD resource planning are challenges that are not encountered by the allies and partners examined in these case studies.
- Other U.S. government agencies have developed tailored approaches and mechanisms that enable budget flexibility and agility to meet mission needs.
- Reinvigorating the defense industrial base is a primary concern for several of the selected countries in these case studies, as well as for the U.S. Department of Energy's National Nuclear Security Administration (NNSA); doing so will require stable and predictable funding over many years and a strategy to manage that base.
- In all these cases, there are complex political, cultural, and historical precedents driving the ability of other countries and other non-DoD agencies to access sufficient resources to fund predicted mission needs in the near and medium terms.
- Among current budget authorities provided by Congress to the selected non-DoD agencies that we examined in Volumes 3 and 6, the U.S. Department of Veterans Affairs (VA)

and NNSA appear to have exceptionally flexible, available authorities that largely insulate them from budget instability and turbulence.

- VA and NNSA are granted special budget authorities by Congress to meet their missions; however, these authorities add to accounting complexities and require accurate predictive modeling.
- There was relatively little indication in the comparative cases of a primary focus on enabling budget agility and flexibility while facilitating innovation or on reducing friction in budget execution; however, these case studies and the United States shared a common focus on the challenge of aligning strategy to budgets.

Contents

Figures and Tables

Figures

Tables

Background and Context

The U.S. Department of Defense's (DoD's) Planning, Programming, Budgeting, and Execution (PPBE) System was first developed in the 1960s as a structured approach for planning long-term resource development, assessing program cost-effectiveness, and aligning resources to strategies. Over the years, changes to the strategic environment, the industrial base, and the nature of military capabilities have raised the question of whether DoD budgeting processes remain well aligned with national security needs.

Congress, in the National Defense Authorization Act for Fiscal Year 2022, called for the establishment of a Commission on PPBE Reform.[1] To fulfill the goals set out by Congress, the commission is conducting a review of lessons from the PPBE-like systems of comparative organizations to improve DoD's PPBE System.

As part of this data collection, the commission asked the National Defense Research Institute, a federally funded research and development center operated by the RAND National Security Research Division, to conduct case studies of budgeting processes first across nine and then eventually across a total of 16 comparative organizations: ten international defense organizations and six U.S. federal government agencies. Congress also specifically requested two case studies of near-peer competitors, and we selected the additional 14 cases in close partnership with the commission. The commission used insights from these analyses to derive lessons for DoD on PPBE reform and convey its recommendations to Congress.

This report is Volume 7 in a seven-volume set of case studies conducted in support of the Commission on PPBE Reform. The accompanying volumes of additional case studies focus on selected U.S. partners and allies (*Planning, Programming, Budgeting, and Execution in Comparative Organizations:* Vol. 5, *Additional Case Studies of Selected Allied and Partner Nations*) and comparable U.S. federal government agencies (*Planning, Programming, Budgeting, and Execution in Comparative Organizations:* Vol. 6, *Additional Case Studies of Selected Non-DoD Federal Agencies*).[2] This volume, an executive summary, distills key insights from these two analytical volumes.

---

[1] Public Law 117-81, National Defense Authorization Act for Fiscal Year 2022, December 27, 2021.

[2] Stephanie Young, Megan McKernan, Andrew Dowse, Nicolas Jouan, Theodora Ogden, Austin Wyatt, Mattias Eken, Linda Slapakova, Naoko Aoki, Clara Le Gargasson, Charlotte Kleberg, Maxime Sommerfeld Antoniou, Phoebe Felicia Pham, Jade Yeung, Turner Ruggi, Erik Silfversten, James Black, Raphael S. Cohen,

Methodology, Limitations, and Caveats

We built our case studies and analyses on five methodological foundations:

- We formed diverse interdisciplinary teams that drew on staff from RAND's U.S. offices, RAND Europe, and RAND Australia, who had direct experience with the comparative organizations that were the focus of the case studies detailed in five of the companion volumes (Volumes 1, 2, 3, 5, and 6) of this report series.[3]
- Acting on guidance from the commission, we developed and used a case-study template and interview protocol to ensure a systematic approach to all the case studies and to facilitate comparisons.
- Literature reviews were extensive and included government documents on budget processes and policies, published academic research, trade literature, and research by international organizations.
- Foreign-language proficiency among the research staff ensured that we could analyze foreign-language sources relevant to the China, France, Germany, Japan, Russia, and Sweden case studies.
- We held more than 160 structured discussions with subject-matter experts and practitioners, including budget officials; staff from the offices of chief financial officers; programmers; and experts from academia, federally funded research and development centers, and think tanks.

All 16 case studies entailed extensive document reviews and structured discussions with subject-matter experts who had experience with the budgeting processes of the international governments and selected U.S. federal government agencies. Each case study was

---

John P. Godges, Heidi Peters, and Lauren Skrabala, *Planning, Programming, Budgeting, and Execution in Comparative Organizations:* Vol. 5, *Additional Case Studies of Selected Allied and Partner Nations*, RAND Corporation, RR-A2195-5, 2024; Stephanie Young, Megan McKernan, Ryan Consaul, Laurinda L. Rohn, Frank G. Klotz, Michael Simpson, Sarah W. Denton, Yuliya Shokh, Madison Williams, Raphael S. Cohen, John P. Godges, Heidi Peters, and Lauren Skrabala, *Planning, Programming, Budgeting, and Execution in Comparative Organizations:* Vol. 6, *Additional Case Studies of Selected Non-DoD Federal Agencies*, RAND Corporation, RR-A2195-6, 2024.

[3] Megan McKernan, Stephanie Young, Timothy R. Heath, Dara Massicot, Mark Stalczynski, Ivana Ke, Raphael S. Cohen, John P. Godges, Heidi Peters, and Lauren Skrabala, *Planning, Programming, Budgeting, and Execution in Comparative Organizations:* Vol. 1, *Case Studies of China and Russia*, RAND Corporation, RR-A2195-1, 2024; Megan McKernan, Stephanie Young, Andrew Dowse, James Black, Devon Hill, Benjamin J. Sacks, Austin Wyatt, Nicolas Jouan, Yuliya Shokh, Jade Yeung, Raphael S. Cohen, John P. Godges, Heidi Peters, and Lauren Skrabala, *Planning, Programming, Budgeting, and Execution in Comparative Organizations:* Vol. 2, *Case Studies of Selected Allied and Partner Nations*, RAND Corporation, RR-A2195-2, 2024; Megan McKernan, Stephanie Young, Ryan Consaul, Michael Simpson, Sarah W. Denton, Anthony Vassalo, William Shelton, Devon Hill, Raphael S. Cohen, John P. Godges, Heidi Peters, and Lauren Skrabala, *Planning, Programming, Budgeting, and Execution in Comparative Organizations:* Vol. 3, *Case Studies of Selected Non-DoD Federal Agencies*, RAND Corporation, RR-A2195-3, 2024; Young, McKernan, Dowse, et al., 2024; Young, McKernan, Consaul, et al., 2024.

assigned a unique team with appropriate regional or organizational expertise. For the near-peer competitor cases (China and Russia), the assigned experts had the language skills and methodological training to work with primary sources in Chinese or Russian. These skills were also required for the cases of international defense organizations of the following countries: France, Germany, Japan, and Sweden. The analysis was also supplemented by experts in the U.S. PPBE process, as applicable. Finally, the RAND research team was led by two researchers who helped ensure that each case study team had some autonomy while maintaining some unity in the overall research approach.

Each case study proceeded in two phases. First, we gathered descriptive content from sources and interviews. Then, we funneled the content into a structured analysis of potential lessons for DoD. Figures 1.1 and 1.2 show the types of information gathered and analyzed in each phase.

We faced three notable limitations in conducting this research. First, the work required detailed analyses of 16 extraordinarily diverse case studies on the tight timeline required by the commission's challenging congressional mandate. Second, all cases presented challenges of data availability—ranging from the opacity of decisionmaking in the near-peer cases to classification issues to differences between formal documentation and how things actually work. Third, the differences and inconsistencies across the cases made it challenging to conduct assessments of cross-case comparability (or comparability with DoD); the international cases involved unique political cultures, governance structures, strategic concerns, and military commitments, while the U.S. agencies had their own unique missions, cultures, resource levels, and congressional oversight.

FIGURE 1.1

Case-Study Descriptive Content Sought in Data Collection

Overview	Planning and Programming	Budgeting and Execution	Oversight
• **Size and nature** of budget • **Key steps** in resource planning (analogous to PPBE processes), including a flow chart • Extent to which **processes are tailored** to certain functions • Factors informing **why the organization has developed** this approach	• **Key stakeholders and participants**; roles and responsibilities • Data and **information management** processes • **Key decision products** • **Tools**; analytic basis for decisionmaking • Tailored processes **for high-tech investments**	• **Degree of fungibility** of resourcing • Organizational **level at which resource decisions are made** (e.g., program, portfolio) • **Processes for changing** planned resource levels • **Feedback mechanisms** to assess the effectiveness of investments	• **Processes** for legislative review, or other forms of oversight • **Key features of oversight**; timeline, key guidance products, mechanisms for changes, rules governing execution • Mechanisms for **reporting and compliance** • Processes for **financial audits**

SOURCE: Reproduced from McKernan, Young, Heath, Massicot, Dowse, et al., 2024, Figure 1.1.

FIGURE 1.2

Case-Study Analysis of Lessons for DoD

Analysis	Target Evaluation Criteria	Insights to Inform DoD's PPBE Process
• **Strengths and weaknesses**, e.g., relative to efficiency, life-cycle planning, flexibility, efficacy of oversights • **Areas for potential U.S. competitive advantage or disadvantage**, relative to adversaries • **Generalizability or applicability** of lessons from each case to other circumstances	• **Thoughtful and responsible use** of resources • **Value to the warfighter** (i.e., does process meet mission needs?) • **Plans linked to budgets** • **Sustained funding** for long-term initiatives • **Flexibility** in case of emerging requirements • Proper **oversight** (or does the process risk misuse of funds?)	• **Lessons for DoD from each case** regarding PPBE • Insights for DoD on how **adversary processes could affect U.S. competitive advantage** • **Caveats and cautions** to inform interpretation

SOURCE: Reproduced from McKernan, Young, Heath, Massicot, Dowse, et al., 2024, Figure 1.2.

In light of these limitations and challenges, any key insights that we derived should be interpreted as perceived strengths, weaknesses, and lessons about an organization in meeting its *own* mission needs. Developing normative judgments about best practices or internally consistent cross-case evaluations is extremely difficult, if only because not all the organizations share the same values or priorities.

Organization of This Report

Chapters 2 and 3 feature the key insights from the allied and partner nation case studies and non-DoD federal agency case studies, respectively, as drawn from the two companion volumes in this report series.[4] This high-level review consolidates the perceived strengths, challenges, and lessons from the two sets of PPBE-like systems examined. Each chapter on key insights includes a discussion of their possible applicability to DoD. These applicability sections speak directly to the commission's mandate—and to the potential utility for DoD's PPBE process. Finally, in Chapter 4, we provide summary tables for the governance and budgetary systems of the near-peer, allied, and partner nations, as well as budgetary flexibilities of comparative U.S. federal agencies.

---

[4] These case studies are fully presented in Young, McKernan, Dowse, et al. (2024) and Young, McKernan, Consaul, et al. (2024).

CHAPTER 2

Key Insights from Additional Case Studies of Allied and Partner Nations

The key insights from the case studies of selected allied and partner nations in Volume 5— France, Germany, Japan, Singapore, and Sweden—are as follows:

- **France, Germany, Japan, Singapore, and Sweden are highly capable U.S. partners that share some strategic concerns and priorities.** The defense priorities of these partners are shaped to a degree by security challenges in Europe and the Indo-Pacific region, which require the countries to develop new capabilities, modernize legacy infrastructure, and boost industrial capacity—all of which entail large financial commitments to defense. This convergence presents opportunities for co-development and broader opportunities to work together toward shared goals, but it also requires the United States and its allies and partners to develop plans and processes to facilitate more-effective approaches to partnership. France, Germany, and Sweden have all demonstrated invigorated commitments to European security and to bolstering and modernizing the North Atlantic Treaty Organization (NATO) alliance in the aftermath of Russia's aggression in Ukraine, while Japan has noted China's rapid military modernization and assertiveness in the region, and Singapore has attempted to retain positive relationships with both the United States and China.
- **Foreign military sales (FMS) are an important mechanism for advancing shared goals, but this support is balanced by initiatives to maintain domestic industrial capacity.** Although all five countries maintain relatively robust industrial capabilities, most also invest in U.S. FMS to strengthen relationships, develop critical capabilities, and foster interconnectedness, interoperability, and interchangeability. Strengthening interoperability is also a key priority for NATO. However, as indicated in these case studies, FMS as a contributor to these objectives needs to be balanced with initiatives to maintain the countries' domestic industrial capabilities.
- **Several countries recently signaled an intent to increase their overall defense spending, but there will be countervailing pressures on top-line budgets.** Complex security challenges have led four of these allies and partners to take concrete steps toward increasing their defense budgets. For the NATO partners, these developments reflect a decade of effort to encourage alliance members to spend at least 2 percent of their gross

domestic product (GDP) on defense. Japan's postwar history has long been defined by a narrow interpretation of its self-defense mission and a self-imposed political constraint on defense spending of no more than 1 percent of GDP. In 2022, it signaled its intention to substantially increase its defense spending via the Defense Buildup Program. However, efforts to increase defense spending will likely face several challenges. There is a question of whether governments can maintain domestic support for more spending on defense, especially if it comes at the risk of tax increases or adding to the public debt.

- **Although the countries' political systems are diverse, there is limited friction between the executive and legislative branches in their budgeting processes.** Despite the diversity of political systems explored in these case studies, interactions between executive and legislative bodies over budgetary priorities appeared to be streamlined, in contrast to the United States. In the Volume 2 analysis of Australia, Canada, and the United Kingdom (UK), we attributed this trend to the parliamentary systems in which the executive had the power of the purse. But, even with the greater diversity in the government structures considered in these five countries, we found that budgets were typically generated in an orderly manner, and in no case did we find examples of budget turbulence emerging from political friction between branches of government to the same degree as is experienced in the United States.

- **The countries place greater emphasis on budget predictability and stability than on agility.** As evidenced throughout their budget processes, these countries prioritize predictability and stability to advance long-term objectives. This stability is seen as a strength to the extent that it offers predictability to industry, enables fiscal planning, and provides steady support for long-term initiatives.

- **Despite the common emphasis on stability, each system provides some budget flexibility to address unanticipated changes.** Several countries have mechanisms for changing budgets during a fiscal year. Singapore and Sweden have provisions for considering supplemental requests. Japan has mechanisms for carrying forward money into the next fiscal year, subject to some constraints. France appears to grant broad authorities for redirecting resources to meet emerging needs; a program manager has mechanisms to move resources within a program or to move resources across programs or even across ministries. Germany's provisions for the transfer of funding (i.e., *virement*) provide flexibility to move resources within the Ministry of Defense budget, subject to threshold requirements and other constraints. Similar to other systems, in Germany, funds can be carried over into the following fiscal year. Several of these cases also include provisions for special funding outside regular budget processes (and fiscal constraints) to support emerging military needs. For example, a special fund was a critical enabler of Germany's support for wartime contingencies in Ukraine and for hitting NATO's spending target, at least in the near term.

- **There are varied approaches to oversight for ensuring transparency, efficiency, and accountability but fewer mechanisms for evaluating effectiveness.** In accordance with their overall structured resource planning processes and generally fiscally conservative policy preferences, most of the countries considered in Volume 5 have robust processes for oversight to ensure that resources are spent as intended. Germany uses regular spending reviews to track performance against established indicators and to ensure that public funds are spent efficiently and effectively. Japan uses both external and internal mechanisms to exercise oversight of government spending, including an independent Board of Audit of Japan. Singapore uses a three-line accountability system that holds individual officials responsible for budgets and relies on internal regulatory processes and internal and external audits for enforcement. However, evaluation processes to assess whether spending has advanced strategic objectives appear to be less mature. This concern seems less applicable to the German system of spending reviews, which reportedly looks at performance toward measurable, impact-based indicators. In the Singapore case, evaluations of spending are conducted largely by the Ministry of Defence, although the Auditor-General leads a limited external review. Singapore relies on its established anti-corruption processes to guard against waste, with audit agencies serving as a backstop.

Applicability of Insights from Case Studies of Allied and Partner Nations

The Commission on PPBE Reform was asked to explore by Congress other PPBE-like processes of selected allied and partner nations to improve DoD's PPBE System. Relative to the UK, Australia, and Canada (considered in Volume 2), the case studies of France, Germany, Japan, Singapore, and Sweden (presented in Volume 5) are more varied and have some notable differences from the United States. For example, the postwar history of Germany and Japan have given these U.S. partners unique political cultures that influence defense spending and the scale of their defense goals, which shape their legal frameworks and domestic politics around resource planning for defense. The pull of domestic politics— alongside geography, history, economics, and other considerations—is evident in threat perceptions in all these cases, as well as the degree of convergence of these countries' perceptions of the strategic environment and defense priorities. We selected these countries, in part, because they maintain significant industrial capacities, but how each country engages with its defense industrial base and decides which capacities and capabilities to maintain varies significantly. There are also significant differences in the sizes of their overall military commitments. For example, the city-state of Singapore might be a highly capable U.S. partner, but it is also small in terms of the monetary value, range, and complexity of its military capabilities.

Despite these differences, we identified the following similarities between these countries and the United States in terms of general approaches to defense resource management:

- Processes are structured and formalized, and they include a variety of well-defined decisionmakers and stakeholders.
- Strategic planning is a key input that is used to explicitly connect priorities to how much is spent to address military threats.
- There are ongoing discussions between the defense organizations and decisionmakers who hold the power of the purse to justify how forces and programs will use their funding.
- Defense organizations receive and spend funding according to agreed-on appropriations rules and then use certain mechanisms, if plans change, to move or carry over funding.
- Oversight is a key mechanism for ensuring that what is budgeted is appropriately spent, even if mechanisms for exercising oversight vary significantly.

It was particularly noteworthy that several features that have been the focus of discussions about the need to reform DoD's PPBE System did not figure prominently in these case studies. For example, the general U.S. focus on potential points of friction between the executive and legislative branches in budget execution—from continuing resolutions to potential government shutdowns and threats of budget sequestration—did not appear to be a significant concern in these cases. Available evidence suggests that levers for reprogramming are manageable and that colors of money and periods of funding availability do not overly constrain the advancement of defense priorities. Likewise, the U.S. focus on processes that foster innovation, agility, and responsiveness to a changing threat environment was not an animating feature in these case studies. Although all the countries had processes to adjust budgets in response to unanticipated contingencies, such as the coronavirus disease 2019 (COVID-19) pandemic or support to Ukraine, they generally placed a high priority on budget stability, predictability, and certainty in their fiscal policies, offering steady signals to industry partners and supporting long-term plans.

CHAPTER 3

Key Insights from Additional Case Studies of Non-DoD Federal Agencies

The key insights from the two case studies of selected non-DoD federal agencies in Volume 6—the U.S. Department of Veterans Affairs (VA) and the U.S. Department of Energy's National Nuclear Security Administration (NNSA)—are as follows:

- **Other U.S. government agencies looked to DoD's PPBE System as a model in developing their own systems, which subsequently evolved.** Both VA and NNSA have looked to DoD's PPBE System as a model for a structured and mature approach to planning and resource allocation decisionmaking. Although the precursor to DoD's PPBE process—the Planning, Programming, and Budgeting System (PPBS)—failed to take hold in VA when originally introduced in the 1960s, some features of a more structured resource planning process, such as a quadrennial review and a five-year financial plan, have been proposed to address perceived shortcomings of VA's existing system. And although the standup of NNSA postdated by several decades the introduction of PPBE to non-DoD agencies, one of its institutional predecessors, the Atomic Energy Commission, was among the agencies that experimented with a resource planning process modeled on DoD's PPBS. Today, NNSA's Office of Cost Estimating and Program Evaluation (CEPE) is also deliberately modeled on DoD's Office of Cost Assessment and Program Evaluation (CAPE).
- **There are perceived opportunities to strengthen connections between strategy and budgets.** In VA, the quadrennial planning process supports development of a strategic plan, but there are perceived opportunities to strengthen how plans drive resource decisionmaking. VA links its annual budget request to mission-oriented outputs (e.g., patients treated, outpatient visits), which, in turn, links resources to mission priorities. At NNSA, the Future Years Nuclear Security Program captures plans beyond the budget year, but there are initiatives to strengthen long-term planning and to better align programs with plans.
- **A variety of mechanisms enable budget flexibility and agility.** VA and NNSA have several budget mechanisms for redirecting appropriated funds. VA's advance appropriations are particularly notable: They can help VA weather the instability from a delayed regular appropriation and position itself for more-stable planning. For NNSA, the lack

of designated types of funding appropriations (*colors of money*), plus the comparatively small number of appropriation accounts, afford more discretion on how to prioritize investments and adjust to meet emerging needs. No-year appropriations enable NNSA to carry over unobligated funds from year to year, allowing the agency to better align appropriated funds to priorities rather than spending one-year appropriations in a rush at the end of a fiscal year. VA also has access to multiyear and no-year appropriations for long-term projects, such as construction and land acquisition. Similar to DoD, VA and NNSA can request congressional approval to reprogram resources to accommodate changes above a given threshold; however, in NNSA at least, this process was reported to be slow and laborious.

- **Mechanisms for enabling agility help agencies weather continuing resolutions and other sources of budget turbulence.** Just as budget flexibilities, such as those cited above, can let a manager decide how to set priorities and where to take risks in light of changing mission needs, they can also help an agency manage under continuing resolutions and mitigate the effects of government shutdowns, such as furloughs. VA's advance appropriations mitigate the challenges of constrained operations under a continuing resolution and of uncertain timing for a regular appropriation. Similarly, NNSA's no-year appropriations provide the agency with a budgetary cushion (and fewer constraints than those faced under a continuing resolution) in the likely event that a regular appropriation is delayed.

- **The emphasis on evaluation rather than execution in some non-DoD PPBE-like processes could be instructive for DoD.** NNSA designates the *E* in PPBE for *evaluation* rather than execution in its process. Thus, in its last PPBE phase, NNSA evaluates progress toward its performance goals. This phase does not generate formal documentation, but its results continuously inform the planning, programming, and budgeting phases. NNSA has developed better analytic inputs in the programming phase to assist with evaluation. For example, NNSA's new FormEX information system and CEPE function have been set up to equip the agency with consistent and rigorous analytic capabilities.

- **Analytical rigor has improved through NNSA's implementation of CAPE-like capabilities.** NNSA has made a substantial effort to centralize its PPBE processes and bolster their rigor by introducing a CAPE-like capability for independent cost estimates and analyses of alternatives through its CEPE office. NNSA has further increased analytical rigor by having its cost analysts report to a single headquarters organization while embedding some of them in NNSA program offices, thus ensuring the use of standardized costing methodologies and improving transparency and alignment of programs to enterprise-wide priorities.

- **Consolidated resource management information systems could improve visibility across the federated structures of government agencies.** NNSA's new FormEX information system reflects an effort to modernize the information technology (IT) infrastructure on which NNSA's PPBE decisions rely. An integrated budget information management system, FormEX provides a common budget structure to facilitate insight into plans, gaps, redundancies, and execution risks. As reflected in DoD's effort (as of 2023) to develop the Advana information system,[1] there are opportunities to leverage IT and data analytics to help make complex decisions, foster stronger transparency, and communicate across stakeholder communities.

Applicability of Insights from Case Studies of Non-DoD Federal Agencies

The Commission on PPBE Reform was asked to explore by Congress other PPBE-like processes of non-DoD federal agencies to improve DoD's PPBE System. Although the budgeting processes were originally modeled after DoD's PPBE System, they have adapted to the unique missions of each agency. Despite the movement away from DoD's PPBE model, the agencies still use similar planning, programming, budgeting, and execution processes. Given these similar processes, there would be no benefit from DoD adopting either of these systems wholesale. However, there is value in exploring the ways in which Congress provides each agency with flexibility so that DoD can ask for similar kinds of flexibility to support more innovation, to make funding more predictable over multiple years, and to obtain relief from various pain points in the system. These pain points include continuing resolutions, rigid appropriation categories, and appropriations for line items instead of portfolios. The commission could further explore the mechanisms for flexibility identified in these two cases.

There are notable similarities in terms of the missions and investment portfolios of VA, NNSA, and DoD. VA, like DoD, provides medical care, builds physical infrastructure, sustains a large footprint of real property, and has ongoing efforts to modernize IT infrastructure. NNSA, like DoD, is required to meet emerging threats in a dynamic, strategic environment and, therefore, needs to enable innovation and leverage new technology. In addition, when defense spending totals are discussed, NNSA funding is part of that number, not just funding for DoD.[2]

However, there are important differences that affect the applicability of lessons learned from VA and NNSA to DoD. As is true for all six case studies of non-DoD organizations when compared with DoD, DoD stands alone in terms of its global roles, the breadth and complexity of its missions, and the overall size of its budget.[3] Both VA and NNSA have more-focused

---

[1] For more on Advana, see Commission on Planning, Programming, Budgeting, and Execution Reform, *Interim Report*, U.S. Senate, August 2023.

[2] The national defense budget function (referred to as function 050) includes the DoD budget (051), atomic energy defense activities (053), and defense-related activities (054). The inclusion of atomic energy defense activities in the national defense budget function predates the creation of NNSA. See, for example, U.S. Government, "Budget FY 1996—Analytical Perspectives, Budget of the United States Government, Fiscal Year 1996," February 1, 1995, Table 6-1, p. 69.

[3] For our analysis of the other four selected non-DoD federal agencies, see Megan McKernan, Stephanie Young, Ryan Consaul, Michael Simpson, Sarah W. Denton, Anthony Vassalo, William Shelton, Devon Hill,

mission sets and significantly smaller discretionary budgets than DoD. Another difference is the overall constitution of the budget portfolios: NNSA does not have mandatory funding, and a large percentage of the VA budget, relative to DoD's budget, consists of mandatory spending. About 40 percent of the VA budget is discretionary spending, and much of this is relatively inflexible because it supports medical care. As a result, resource planning depends more on actuarial modeling in VA than in DoD. This difference in planning and programming approaches reflects VA's unique mission and budget portfolio.

Raphael S. Cohen, John P. Godges, Heidi Peters, and Lauren Skrabala, *Planning, Programming, Budgeting, and Execution in Comparative Organizations:* Vol. 3, *Case Studies of Selected Non-DoD Federal Agencies,* RAND Corporation, RR-A2195-3, 2024.

CHAPTER 4

Summary of Cross-Case Insights

Summary of Defense Governance and Budgetary Systems of the United States and Comparative Nations

In Tables 4.1 through 4.10, we summarize the defense governance and budgetary systems of the assessed near-peer, allied, and partner nations, compared with U.S. defense governance and budgetary systems. These tables are organized first by governance systems (Tables 4.1 and 4.2) and then by the four budgetary functions of planning (Tables 4.3 and 4.4), programming (Tables 4.5 and 4.6), budgeting (Tables 4.7 and 4.8), and execution (Tables 4.9 and 4.10).[1]

TABLE 4.1

Governance: U.S. and Comparative Nation Government Structures and Key Participants

Country	Structure of Government or Political System	Key Governing Bodies and Participants
United States	Federal presidential constitutional republic	• President of the United States • Office of Management and Budget (OMB) • Congress (House of Representatives and Senate) • U.S. Department of Defense (DoD) • Secretary of Defense and senior DoD leadership • Joint Chiefs of Staff
China	Unitary one-party socialist republic	• Politburo Standing Committee • National People's Congress (NPC) • Central Military Commission (CMC)
Russia	Federal semi-presidential republic	• President of Russia • Federal Assembly (State Duma and the Federation Council) • President's Security Council • Ministry of Defense (MoD) • Military-Industrial Commission (VPK) • Rostec (Russian state-owned defense conglomerate headquartered in Moscow)

---

[1] Information in these tables is derived from multiple sources and materials cited in Volumes 1, 2, and 5. For full bibliographic details, see McKernan, Young, Heath, Massicot, Stalczynski, et al. (2024); McKernan, Young, Dowse, et al. (2024); and Young, McKernan, Dowse, et al. (2024).

Table 4.1—Continued

Country	Structure of Government or Political System	Key Governing Bodies and Participants
Australia	Federal parliamentary constitutional monarchy	• Prime minister • Governor-general • Parliament (House of Representatives and Senate) • Minister for Defence • Department of Defence
Canada	Federal parliamentary constitutional monarchy	• Prime minister • Governor general • Parliament (House of Commons and Senate) • Department of National Defence (DND) • Minister of Finance • Minister of National Defence • Deputy Minister of National Defence
UK	Unitary parliamentary constitutional monarchy	• Prime minister • Parliament (House of Commons and House of Lords) • Ministry of Defence (MoD) • Secretary of State for Defence • Permanent Under-Secretary of State for Defence
France	Unitary semi-presidential republic	• President • Prime minister • Parliament (National Assembly and Senate) • National Defense and Security Council • Ministry of the Economy, Finance and Digital Sovereignty (MinFin) • Ministry of Armed Forces (MinArm), including the Chief of Defense Staff (CEMA) and the Directorate General of Armament (DGA) • Armament Engineering Corps
Germany	Federal parliamentary republic	• Federal President • Chancellor • Parliament (Bundestag and Bundesrat) • Federal Ministry of Defense • Federal Ministry of Finance (BMF) and Ministry of Economic Affairs • Bundeswehr (German armed forces) • Chief of Defense (also known as the Inspector General)
Japan	Unitary parliamentary constitutional monarchy	• Prime minister • Diet (House of Representatives and House of Councillors) • Council on Economic and Fiscal Policy • Cabinet • Ministry of Finance • Ministry of Defense (MOD), inclusive of the Self-Defense Forces (SDF)

Table 4.1—Continued

Country	Structure of Government or Political System	Key Governing Bodies and Participants
Singapore	Unitary dominant-party parliamentary republic	• Prime minister • President, as the "fiscal guardian" of government funds • Parliament (unicameral) • Cabinet-level Minister for Defence • Ministry of Defence (MINDEF), inclusive of the Singapore Armed Forces (SAF) • Two Civilian Permanent Secretary for Defence positions: the Permanent Secretary (Defence) and the Permanent Secretary (Defence Development) • Chief of Defence Force
Sweden	Unitary parliamentary constitutional monarchy	• Prime minister • Riksdag (parliament) • Defence Commission • Cabinet-level ministries, including the Ministry of Defence (inclusive of a Minister for Defence, responsible for military defense, and a Minister for Civil Defence, responsible for crisis preparedness and civil defense) • 12 defense-oriented civilian-led government agencies, independent of the Ministry of Defence, including the Swedish Armed Forces (SwAF), the Defence Materiel Administration, and the Defence Research Agency • Supreme Commander of the SwAF, or the Chief of Defence • Civilian Director-General (responsible for logistics and finances)

TABLE 4.2

Governance: U.S. and Comparative Nation Spending Controls and Decision Support Systems

Country	Control of Government Spending	Decision Support Systems
United States	Legislative review and approval of executive budget proposal	• Planning, Programming, Budgeting, and Execution (PPBE) System • Joint Capabilities Integration and Development System (JCIDS) • Defense Acquisition System (DAS)
China	Executive with nominal legislative review and approval	• 2019 Defense White Paper indicated adoption of "demand-oriented planning" and "planning-led" resource allocation
Russia	Executive with assessed nominal legislative review and approval	• Unclear

Table 4.2—Continued

Country	Control of Government Spending	Decision Support Systems
Australia	Executive with legislative review and approval. Appropriations legislation must originate in the House of Representatives; Senate may reject legislation but cannot amend it.	One Defense Capability System (ODCS), including the following: • the Integrated Force Design Process, featuring a two-year cycling Defense Capability Assessment Program (DCAP) • the Integrated Investment Program (IIP), which documents planned future capability investments and informs the Portfolio Budget Statement, the proposed allocation of resources to outcomes • acquisition of approved IIP capability programs • sustainment and disposal of capability programs.
Canada	Executive with assessed limited influence of legislative review and approval	• Expenditure Management System • Defence Capabilities Board • Independent Review Panel for Defence Acquisition
UK	Executive with legislative review and approval	• Public Finance Management Cycle • Planning, Budgeting, and Forecasting (PB&F) • Defence Operating Model
France	Executive with nominal legislative approval and input	• Planning and programming processes rooted in defense strategic guidance that generates a long-term defense spending plan executed through annual budgets
Germany	Executive with strong legislative review and approval	• Planning and programming processes, inclusive of the Integrated Planning Process, rooted in defense strategic guidance that generates a defense spending plan executed through annual budgets
Japan	Executive with legislative review and approval	• Planning and programming processes rooted in defense strategic guidance • 3-year time frame for budget formulation, execution, and settlement, with formulation beginning approximately 1 year before a new fiscal year and settlement of accounts 1 year after execution time frame
Singapore	Executive with nominal legislative approval	• Exact nature and processes associated with decision support systems are opaque in open-source materials; sources suggest that analogous processes exist at the MINDEF level, with some level of review and approval for certain decisions—such as procurement decisions—provided by the Minister for Defence.
Sweden	Executive through collective decisionmaking at the ministerial level, with legislative review and approval	• Historical use of a System for Finance, Planning, and Economic Management patterned after U.S. PPBE system, with defense planning and budgeting the responsibility of the SwAF (with limited input from parliament) • Financial crisis of early 1990s resulted in major reforms, such as the introduction of a Defence Commission, which serves as a consensus-building forum on Swedish defense policy between the government and representatives from parliament. • Other reforms introduced a client-contractor model of outlays, whereby SwAF procures services from other government agencies.

TABLE 4.3

Planning: U.S. and Comparative Nation Inputs and Outputs

Country	Key Planning Inputs	Selected Planning Outputs
United States	• National Security Strategy • National Defense Strategy • National Military Strategy	• Chairman's Program Recommendations • Defense Planning Guidance • Fiscal Guidance
China	• Five-Year Programs • Military Strategic Guidelines • Other multiyear plans (People's Liberation Army [PLA] five-year professional development plans, etc.) • Annual PLA budget requirements	• Outline of the Five-Year Program for Military Development • Military components of other multiyear plans • Annual PLA budgets
Russia	• State Armaments Program (SAP) procurement plan	• State Defense Order (SDO)
Australia	• 2016 Defence White Paper • 2017 Defence Industry Policy Statement • 2017 Strategy Framework • 2019 Defence Policy for Industry Participation • 2020 Defence Strategic Update • 2020 Force Structure Plan • 2023 Defence Strategic Review • Defence Planning Guidance/Chief of the Defence Force Preparedness Directive (Not available to the general public) • Other strategic plans and documents outlining planning and program requirements	• IIP for future capability investment
Canada	• 2017 defence white paper (*Strong, Secure, Engaged*) • 2018 Defence Plan, 2018–2023 • 2019 Defence Investment Plan • 2020 Defence Capabilities Blueprint (updated monthly) • 2022 Department of National Defence and Canadian Armed Forces Engagement Plan (released annually)	• Annual department plans to link DND strategic priorities and expected program results to the Main Estimates presented to parliament
UK	• Public Finance Management Cycle • PB&F • Defence Operating Model	• 2021 Defence Command Paper (*Defence in a Competitive Age*) aligns MoD priorities with the Integrated Review • 2021 Defence and Security Industrial Strategy
France	• 2022 Strategic Review of Defense and National Security	• Nonbinding Military Programming Law (LPM), which determines a 4–7-year defense budget spending plan
Germany	• 2016 white paper • 2022 *Zeitenwende* speech from Chancellor Olaf Scholz	• 2018 Concept of implementation for white paper–articulated key aims of the Bundeswehr • 2023 National Security Strategy
Japan	• National Security Strategy (NSS) • National Defense Strategy (NDS)	• Defense Buildup Program

Table 4.3—Continued

Country	Key Planning Inputs	Selected Planning Outputs
Singapore	• No public release of defense strategic documents or plans in recent years; closest analog is an articulated commitment to dual pillars of diplomacy and deterrence.	• Sources suggest that Singapore has embarked on a modernization and investment plan to achieve a "Next Generation SAF."
Sweden	• Articulated commitment to "total defense" and forward-looking operational and investment plans • Armed Forces Development Plan recommending options to improve Swedish defense capabilities over a 10-year window • SwAF annual report summarizing previous year's performance	• Documents such as the 2022 Materiel Supply Strategy • Parliament-approved defense bill providing overall strategic direction for Swedish defense (approved every 5 years), with directives implemented annually • Annual budget bill

TABLE 4.4

Planning: U.S. and Comparative Nation Strategic Emphasis and Stakeholders

Country	Strategic Planning Emphasis	Planning Stakeholders
United States	2022 National Defense Strategy highlights four priorities: (1) defending the United States, "paced to the growing multi-domain threat posed by the PRC"; (2) deterring "strategic attacks against the United States, Allies, and partners"; (3) deterring aggression and being prepared to "prevail in conflict when necessary," with priority placed first on the People's Republic of China "challenge in the Indo-Pacific region" and then "the Russia challenge in Europe"; and (4) "building a resilient Joint Force and defense ecosystem."	• Under Secretary of Defense for Policy (lead actor, produces Defense Planning Guidance) • President (National Security Strategy, Fiscal Guidance) • Secretary of Defense (National Defense Strategy, Fiscal Guidance at DoD level) • Chairman of the Joint Chiefs of Staff (CJCS) (National Military Strategy, Chairman's Program Recommendations)
China	Focused, long-term investment for priority projects of high strategic value	• Central Chinese Communist Party leadership • National People's Congress • State Council • Defense-related state-owned enterprises • CMC, senior military leadership
Russia	Closely linked to strategy and national security threats with a recent emphasis on modernization; assessed to be, in part, aspirational	• MoD • Central Research Institute • VPK, representing Rostec, defense industry, and national security agencies
Australia	2023 Defence Strategic Review emphasized a strategy of deterrence to deny an adversary freedom of action to militarily coerce Australia and to operate against Australia without being held at risk	• Strategic guidance generated by Department of Defence; approved by the Minister for Defence • IIP managed by the Vice Chief of the Defence Force, with input from stakeholders and joint strategic planning units, such as the Force Design Division

Table 4.4—Continued

Country	Strategic Planning Emphasis	Planning Stakeholders
Canada	2017 white paper emphasized three components to Canadian national defense: (1) defense of national sovereignty through Canadian Armed Forces capable of assisting in response to natural disasters, search and rescue, and other emergencies; (2) defense of North America through partnership with the United States in the North American Aerospace Defense Command (NORAD); and (3) international engagements, including through peace support operations and peacekeeping.	• DND and supporting cabinet entities
UK	2021 Defence Command Paper emphasized seven primary goals of the MoD and the British Armed Forces: (1) defense of the UK and its overseas territories, (2) sustainment of UK nuclear deterrence capacity, (3) global influence projection, (4) execution of North Atlantic Treaty Organization (NATO) responsibilities, (5) promotion of national prosperity, (6) peacekeeping contributions, and (7) supporting defense and intelligence-gathering capabilities of UK allies and partners.	• Prime minister's Cabinet Office (Integrated Review) • MoD (Defense Command Paper and other strategic documents)
France	• As of the 2022 Strategic Review, strategic concerns include intensification of strategic competition, the increased fragility of collective security, and the diversification of means of intimidation and aggression. • 2024–2030 LPM has stated aims that are to (1) maintain the credibility of French military nuclear deterrence; (2) reinforce resilience and assert sovereignty within France's territories, particularly its overseas territories; (3) defend common spaces (cyberspace, space, the seabed, and air-maritime spaces); and (4) rethink and diversify strategic partnerships, so as to reinforce France's capacity to influence, prevent, and intervene beyond its borders, as well as reinforce its capacity to lead large missions with partners and allies if necessary.	• President, supported by the Minister of the Armed Forces and the National Defense and Security Council

Table 4.4—Continued

Country	Strategic Planning Emphasis	Planning Stakeholders
Germany	• National Security Strategy echoes themes of the *Zeitenwende* speech, identifying Russia as the current significant threat to peace and security in the Euro-Atlantic area; notes that China must be viewed as a partner in addition to a competitor and systemic rival; highlights the risks represented by fragile states and internal conflicts within the "neighborhood" of Europe; and flags the "complex threats" represented by terrorism, organized crime, cyberattacks, and illegal financial flows. • National Security Strategy articulates an "integrated security" for Germany that features (1) robust defense of German and European peace and freedom; (2) defense of Germany's free democratic order against illegitimate foreign interference, disinformation, and extremism; and (3) safeguarding natural resources through such efforts as climate-crisis adaptation strategies, strengthening of global food security, and preventing future global pandemics.	• Federal Ministry of Defense
Japan	• 2022 NSS identified growing threats from China, North Korea, and Russia as key challenges and articulated a requirement for "comprehensive national power" containing diplomatic, defensive, economic, technological, and intelligence capabilities, including significant new defense capabilities. • 2022 NDS reiterates "three pillars" of Japan's defense architecture (SDF capability, alliance with the United States, and security cooperation with partners and allies) and articulates seven key capability priorities that will support its strategic objectives: (1) standoff capabilities, (2) integrated air and missile defense, (3) uncrewed systems, (4) cross-domain capabilities, (5) command and control and intelligence, (6) mobility, and (7) sustainability and resilience.	• MOD • Defense Minister • Prime minister
Singapore	• Diplomacy pillar looks to state diplomacy and the international rules-based order to protect Singaporean interests and build diplomatic strategic depth. • Deterrence pillar looks to emphasize Singapore's ability to maintain stability and security by possessing an ability to credibly deter potential aggressors.	• Defence Policy Office (DPO) under the Deputy Secretary (Policy) to the Permanent Secretary (Defence) leads defense planning, with key decisions made by the Minister for Defence and other cabinet-level officials
Sweden	• National defense policy that centers on "total defense," an all-of-society national defense effort that includes military, civil, economic, and psychological elements, including the fundamental importance of endurance and an aim of being able to withstand a crisis for at least 3 months	• SwAF and Ministry of Defence component agencies • Parliament

TABLE 4.5

Programming: U.S. and Comparative Nation Resource Allocations and Time Frames

Country	Resource Allocation Decisions	Programming Time Frame
United States	Documented in Program Objective Memorandum (POM) developed by DoD components, reflecting a "systematic analysis of missions and objectives to be achieved, alternative methods of accomplishing them, and the effective allocation of the resources," and reviewed by the Director of Cost Assessment and Program Evaluation (CAPE)	• 5 years
China	Top-down planning from CMC services and commands supplemented by bottom-up requirements submitted by military unit financial departments	• 5 years, sometimes longer
Russia	Top-down planning from Ministry of Defense for the SDO, the annual appropriation for military procurement to meet the requirements of the SAP	• 3 years; nominal 10-year SAP, revised within 5 years in practice
Australia	Portfolio Budget Statement (as informed by the IIP) for the current fiscal year	Three-tiered funding stream that provides • current fiscal year funding • forward-looking estimates with a high degree of confidence for the next 3 fiscal years • provisional funding with a medium degree of confidence for the next 10 years, as articulated in the IIP and defense strategic guidance documents.
Canada	Government Expenditure Plan and Main Estimates allocate budget resources to departments and programs.	• 3 years, as articulated in the Annual Department Plan
UK	• Main supply estimates (MEs) for the current fiscal year, based on spending limits set in the Integrated Review, and additional estimates for 10 years out as articulated in the MoD *Defence Equipment Plan*, which is updated annually • Supplementary supply estimates (SEs) allow MoD to request additional resources, capital, or cash for the current fiscal year. • Excess votes—although discouraged—allow retroactive approval of overruns from a prior fiscal year, because government departments cannot legally spend more money than has been approved by parliament.	• 3–5 years, as articulated in the Integrated Review, which provides medium-term financial planning
France	Dialogue between the CEMA and DGA within the MinArm to make resource allocation decisions, informed through engagement with the MinFin, with disagreements resolved by the president in consultation with the National Defense and Security Council	• 4–7 years, as articulated in the LPM
Germany	Bundeswehr Office for Defense Planning delivers integrated planning within a 15-year horizon.	• 5 years under the federal financial plan

Table 4.5—Continued

Country	Resource Allocation Decisions	Programming Time Frame
Japan	Top-down resource allocations decisions, with characteristics of a strategies-to-task framework, inclusive of input from staff offices	• 10 years, separated into two 5-year epochs
Singapore	Internal SAF review and prioritization of capability gaps: service branches bring capability gaps to the DPO, which conducts initial prioritization of service branch requests, with prioritized capability gaps examined by the Systems Integration Office, then reviewed by the DPO, with final approval provided by the Minister for Defence	• Rolling 5-year capability acquisition plans of each SAF service branch
Sweden	SwAF, with review and approval by parliament	• 10-year operational plan (FMVP) and 12-year investment plan, reviewed and approved by parliament every 5 years in defense bills • Budget framework projecting 3 years into the future with annual updates

TABLE 4.6

Programming: U.S. and Comparative Nation Stakeholders

Country	Programming Stakeholders
United States	• Director, CAPE (lead actor, provides analytic baseline to analyze the POM produced by DoD components, leads program reviews, forecasts resource requirements, and updates the Future Years Defense Program [FYDP]) • DoD components (produce POM, document proposed resource requirements for programs over 5-year timespan, which comprises the FYDP) • CJCS (assesses component POMs, provides chairman's program assessment reflecting the extent to which the military departments [MILDEPs] have satisfied combatant command [COCOM] requirements) • Deputy Secretary of Defense (adjudicates disputes through the Deputy's Management Action Groups) • Secretary of Defense (as needed, directs DoD components to execute Resource Management Decision memorandums to reflect decisionmaking during the programming and budget phases)
China	• Ministry of Finance National Defense Department • CMC Logistics Support Department • CMC Strategic Planning Office
Russia	• Ministry of Finance • Ministry of Economic Development • MoD • President's Security Council • VPK

Table 4.6—Continued

Country	Programming Stakeholders
Australia	• At Department of Defence level, decisionmaking for resources made through Defence Committee (Defence Secretary, Chief of the Defence Force, Vice Chief of the Defence Force, Associate Defence Secretary, Chief Finance Officer) • Capability-related submissions reviewed by Minister for Finance–led National Security Investment Committee of Cabinet • Approved by National Security Committee (prime minister, deputy prime minister, Minister for Defence, Treasurer, Minister for Finance, other ministers when necessary)
Canada	• Treasury Board and Department of Finance (sets annual spending limits for federal agencies that are applicable to capital expenditures and determines the number of new projects funded) • Department of Finance, led by the Minister of Finance (drafts budget for presentation to parliament) • Minister of Finance and prime minister have approval authority. • Assistant Deputy Minister for Finance, DND and the DND Finance Group (prepares DND budget and liaises with Treasury Board Secretariat, Department of Finance, and other federal agencies) • Military service comptrollers
UK	• Component entities negotiate with MoD through "demand" signals; components program against required outputs. • MoD reviews and prioritizes proposed programs through a centralized process. • MoD Director General, Finance, working with the Deputy Chief of the Defense Staff for Military Capability (part of the MoD Financial and Military Capability team) • Supported by Director of Financial Planning and Scrutiny and the Assistant Chief of the Defence Staff for Capability and Force Design (part of the Financial and Military Capability team) • Process execution delegated to the Head of Defence Resources
France	• MinArm, including the CEMA, DGA, and Secretary-General for Administration • MinFin • Prime minister • President
Germany	• Bundeswehr Office for Defense Planning (delivers integrated planning within a 15-year horizon)
Japan	• MOD internal bureaus • MOD staff offices • Acquisition, Technology, and Logistics Agency

Singapore	• Minister for Defence
	• Under the MINDEF:
	  – SAF service branches
	  – DPO
	  – Weapons Staff Officers of the Systems Integration Office
	  – Defense Technology Community, including various organizations, such as the Future Systems and Technology Directorate (FSTD), the Defence Science and Technology Agency (DSTA), and the Defence Science Organisation National Laboratories (DSO)

Sweden	• SwAF • Parliament

TABLE 4.7

Budgeting: U.S. and Comparative Nation Time Frames and Major Categories

Country	Budget Approval Time Frames	Major Budget Categories
United States	Annual	• 5 categories: Military Personnel (MILPERS); Operations and Maintenance (O&M); Procurement; Research, Development, Test, and Evaluation (RDT&E); and Military Construction (MILCON)
China	Annual	• 3 reported categories in defense white papers: personnel, armaments, and maintenance and operations
Russia	Annual	• 9 categories: Armed Forces of the Russian Federation, Modernization of the Armed Forces, Mobilization and Pre-Conscription Training, Mobilization of the Economy, Participation in Collective Peacekeeping Agreements, Nuclear Weapons Complex, International Military-Technical Cooperation, Research and Development, and a category designated for Other Expenditures
Australia	• Annual, with separate appropriations bills for existing services and programs and for new programs • Accrual budgeting with budget request covering ongoing costs; associated funding cannot be carried over to the next fiscal year	• 5 categories: Workforce, Operations, Capability Acquisition Programs (including research and development), Capability Sustainment, and Operating Costs
Canada	Annual; disbursement of funds made through 3 supply periods, each reviewed and approved by parliament with Main Estimates and Supplementary Estimate A (i.e., spending not ready to be included in a Main Estimate at time of preparation) presented in first supply period. Supplementary Estimate B is presented in the second supply period, and Supplementary Estimate C (as needed) is presented in the third supply period.	• Various categories: votes for separate tranches of funding roughly correspond to DoD's *colors of money.* FY 2022–FY 2023 contained four votes for (1) operating expenditures; (2) capital expenditures, including major capability programs and infrastructure projects; (3) grants and contributions, including payments to NATO and funding for partner-nation military programs; and (4) payments for long-term disability and life insurance plans for Canadian Armed Forces Members. • Main Estimates also categorize spending by purpose. FY 2022–FY 2023 purpose categorizations include such areas as (1) ready forces, (2) capability procurement, (3) future force design, and (4) operations.
UK	Annual	• 8 categories: as split by the MoD for its internal PPBE-like process, corresponding to 8 main MoD organizations, central oversight to promote jointness • Budgets divided into commodity blocks (capital departmental expenditure limit for investment, resource departmental expenditure limit for current costs, etc.) and by activity (personnel, etc.)

Table 4.7—Continued

Country	Budget Approval Time Frames	Major Budget Categories
France	Annual	• Under Organic Law Relating to Finance Laws or LOLF, mission-based budget is subdivided into programs: Current defense budget includes 3 missions and 8 key programs, which can be divided further into spending associated with specific actions, subactions, and operations. • Defense mission, inclusive of (1) Program 144, Environment and Future Defense Policy; (2) Program 146, Equipment of the Armed Forces; (3) Program 178, Preparation and Employment of forces; and (4) Program 212, Support to the Defense Policy • Veterans, Remembrance, and Defense-Nation Links mission, inclusive of (1) Program 158, Compensation for Victims of Anti-Semitic Persecution and Acts of Barbarism During World War II and (2) Program 169, Recognition and Compensation for Veterans • Economic Recovery Plan mission, inclusive of (1) Program 362, Ecology, and (2) Program 363, Competitiveness
Germany	Annual	• 11 categories: (1) command authorities and troops, social security contributions, welfare measures, and support for soldiers; (2) accommodation; (3) Federal Armed Forces administration, Federal Armed Forces universities, and military chaplaincy; (4) maintenance of Bundeswehr equipment; (5) other Bundeswehr operations; (6) military procurement; (7) centrally budgeted administrative income and expenses; (8) NATO and other international institutions-related commitments, as well as measures related to international operations; (9) military research, development, and testing; (10) Federal Office for the Military Counterintelligence Services (counterterrorism operations); and (11) other appropriations (disaster relief efforts)
Japan	Annual; cash-basis accounting	• 7 categories: (1) standoff capabilities, (2) integrated air and missile defense, (3) uncrewed systems, (4) cross-domain capabilities, (5) command and control and intelligence, (6) mobility, and (7) sustainability and resilience

Table 4.7—Continued

Country	Budget Approval Time Frames	Major Budget Categories
Singapore	Annual; cash-basis accounting	• Government spending categorized under security and external relations, social development, government administration, and economic development • All government spending also divided into operating and development expenditure categories • For MINDEF, operating expenditure categories include personnel, operations, maintenance, and procurement, with development expenditures linked to long-term investments in capital assets, infrastructure, and land development. • MINDEF colors of money analogs include investments in human capital (personnel training and salaries), operating and development (readiness and international deployments), and investments in new capabilities (procurement and research and development [R&D])
Sweden	Annual, with the Spring Fiscal Policy Bill outlining maximum spending for the government in the subsequent 3 fiscal years that updates the multiyear budget framework, and a Fall Budget Bill that finalizes cabinet-level negotiations of division of approved funding between 27 expenditure areas	• 9 categories under Expenditure Area 6, "Defense and Society's Preparedness": (1) unit activities and preparedness, (2) state pension fees, (3) maintenance of equipment and facilities, (4) military intelligence and security service, (5) armed international operations of the SwAF, (6) other international operations of the SwAF, (7) acquisition of equipment and facilities, (8) research and technology development, and (9) the SwAF

TABLE 4.8

Budgeting: Selected U.S. and Comparative Nation Stakeholders

Country	Selected Budgeting Stakeholders
United States	DoD • Under Secretary of Defense (Comptroller) • DoD components and COCOMs Executive Branch • OMB Congress • House Budget Committee • Senate Budget Committee • House Appropriations Committee (Defense Subcommittee) • Senate Appropriations Committee (Defense Subcommittee) • House Armed Services Committee • Senate Armed Services Committee
China	• State Council • NPC • NPC Standing Committee • NPC Finance and Economic Committee

Table 4.8—Continued

Country	Selected Budgeting Stakeholders
Russia	• Ministry of Finance • Ministry of Economic Development • MoD • President • Federal Assembly (State Duma and the Federation Council) • Accounts Chamber
Australia	Department of Defence management: • Vice Chief of the Defence Force • Associate Secretary of Defence • Investment Committee (chaired by the Vice Chief of the Defence Force, makes departmental decisions associated with execution of the IIP) • Capability managers (senior military officials, Chief Defence Scientist, CIO, and the Deputy Secretary Security and Estate) and lead delivery groups Decisions are ultimately the responsibility of the civilian executive government (prime minister, cabinet).
Canada	• Treasury Board and Department of Finance • Assistant Deputy Minister for Finance, DND and the DND Finance Group • Military service comptrollers
UK	• His Majesty's (HM) Treasury sets annual limits on net spending. • MoD drafts and presents MEs and SEs to parliament at different points within the fiscal-year cycle, in close coordination with HM Treasury. • House of Commons Defence Select Committee examines MEs; parliament votes on MEs and SEs. • MoD Director General, Finance, working with the Deputy Chief of the Defense Staff for Military Capability (part of the MoD Financial and Military Capability team) • Supported by Director of Financial Planning and Scrutiny and the Assistant Chief of the Defence Staff for Capability and Force Design (part of the Financial and Military Capability team) • Process execution is delegated to the Head of Defence Resources.
France	• MinArm, including CEMA and DGA • MinFin • Parliament (National Assembly and Senate) • High Council of Public Finances • Council of State • Prime minister • President
Germany	• Tax estimation generated by representatives from the BMF, the Ministry of Economic Affairs, other federal ministries, and the Deutsches Bundesbank and experts from six research institutes • BMF provides budget baseline. • Ministry of Defense submits financial needs and outlines policy priorities to the BMF. • Defense Ministry Budget and Oversight Department • Bundestag and Bundesrat review and amend BMF-submitted federal budget.
Japan	• MOD internal bureaus • Ministry of Finance Budget Bureau (collects budget requests from ministries and incorporates them into a budgetary framework, with negotiations and adjustments as needed) • Council on Economic and Fiscal Policy (sets policy guidelines for spending in the next fiscal year by issuing the Basic Policy on Economic and Fiscal Management and Reform) • Direction, approval, and political influence exerted by the prime minister, cabinet, and members of the Diet, with informal communication between stakeholders used to build consensus and resolve differences

Table 4.8—Continued

Country	Selected Budgeting Stakeholders
Singapore	• Under MINDEF, the Defence Management Group's Defence Finance Organisation is responsible for managing the defense budget and long-range planning.
Sweden	• SwAF • Parliament

TABLE 4.9

Execution: U.S. and Comparative Nation Budgetary Flexibilities and Reprogramming

Country	Budgetary Flexibilities and Reprogramming
United States	• Funding availability varies by account type; multiyear or no-year appropriations for limited programs as authorized by Congress • Limited carryover authority in accordance with OMB Circular A-11 • Reprogramming as authorized; four defined categories of reprogramming actions, including prior-approval reprogramming actions—increasing procurement quantity of a major end item, establishing a new program, etc.—which require approval from congressional defense committees • Transfers as authorized through general and special transfer authorities, typically provided in defense authorization and appropriations acts
China	• Some flexibility extended to lower-level decisionmakers to adjust spending and acquisitions; further specifics unclear
Russia	• Signed contract timelines shorter than SAP timelines; provides some degree of flexibility to MoD to realign procurements with changing strategic goals; further specifics unclear
Australia	• Ten-year indicative baseline for defense spending (except operating costs) provides budgetary certainty entering into each new fiscal year. • IIP includes approved capability development programs—for which funding does not expire—and unapproved programs that can be accelerated or delayed as needs arise or change to reallocate funds through biannual review process overseen by the Vice Chief of the Defence Force, including between services and for new projects • IIP is 20% overprogrammed for acquisition to manage risks of underachievement or overexpenditure relative to the acquisition budget. • Funding for operations, sustainment, and personnel is separate from the IIP. • Capability managers have a high degree of flexibility for spending allocated operating funds; responsible for achieving outcomes articulated in the Portfolio Budget Statement.
Canada	• Organizations can transfer funds within a vote from one program to another without parliament's approval. • Organizations do need parliament's approval to transfer funds between votes. • Canadian federal agencies allowed to carry forward a portion of unspent funds for a fiscal year—typically up to 5% of operating expenditures and 20% of capital expenditures. • Government can authorize continued spending at prior-year levels if a budget has not been passed by parliament by the beginning of the fiscal year. • Special warrants can be issued to fund continued normal government operations if a government falls and an election is called before a budget can be passed; this can also be used on a short-term basis to avoid the need for a parliament vote on funding. • Interim supply bill for a new fiscal year is typically presented and voted on in third supply period of prior fiscal year to allow continued government operations; the budget and Main Estimates are introduced close to the beginning of a new fiscal year.

Table 4.9—Continued

Country	Budgetary Flexibilities and Reprogramming
UK	• Defense operations funded separately through HM Treasury or (in certain circumstances) UK Integrated Security Fund (as managed by the Cabinet Office's) Joint Funds Unit • Already voted funding can be moved within top-line budget programs with HM Treasury approval, provided they remain in the same commodity block • MoD funds can also be directly transferred between programs within a departmental expenditure limit or annual managed expenditure in a process known as *virement*, subject to restrictions. • Additional funding for one or more top-line budget programs can be requested from parliament as an SE. • Portions of budget subject to highest degree of fluctuation treated as annual managed expenditures (with operations covered through HM Treasury and/or UK Integrated Security Fund); MoD can request additional funds from HM Treasury to support urgent and unanticipated needs.
France	• At the program level: – Specific mechanisms include fungibility at the program level allowing program manager to allocate "credits" between different operations provided the ceiling for personnel expenditure is not exceeded (although credits for personnel expenditures can be redistributed to operational expenses) – Distribution of additional credits – Virements of credits across programs within the same ministry (with prime minister decree on the advice of MinFin) – Transfer of credits across programs and ministries (with prime minister decree on the advice of MinFin) – Additional funds generated through such mechanisms as licensing of state-held intellectual property rights – Use of a precautionary reserve, which requires programs to save a fraction of allocated credits in order to respond to future unexpected events • At the finance law level: – Specific mechanisms include amendments to the finance law, provision of advanced emergency funding from the next fiscal year's finance law, reallocation of funding across ministries to support the defense mission, or creation of a new finance law
Germany	• Bundeswehr special fund (Sondervermögen)—a type of German public financing used for programs or projects with defined objectives and predetermined timelines—with current objectives that include strengthening alliance and defense capabilities and financing significant equipment projects in order to reach an average of 2% of GDP spending on defense within a 5-year period • Flexibility in disbursing funds to purposes other than those intended, as long as total spending does not exceed funding allocated to each ministry • No limits associated on virement within chapters; 20% allowance for transfer of funds between chapters—transfers above 20% threshold require BMF approval • Funds can be carried over into next fiscal year without a specified limit in situations in which (1) there is a contractual obligation to do so or (2) it is authorized by Bundestag and promotes "efficient and economical use" of the carryover funds.
Japan	• 3 mechanisms for obtaining additional funding: (1) supplementary budget, compiled by the cabinet and submitted to the Diet for approval; (2) use of emergency reserve funds included in the main budget for contingencies, with cabinet approval; and (3) reallocation of funds, through (a) changing budget implementation plan or (b) reallocating funds within the same budget subcategory • Use of multiyear contractual commitments • Authority to carry over funds through four mechanisms: (1) direct carry forward of unspent allocated funds, with Diet approval; (2) carryover of unspent funds resulting from accidents or external shocks; (3) continuation expenses for a multiyear project; and (4) special account budgets, which are separate from the general account budget and used to manage specific programs

Table 4.9—Continued

Country	Budgetary Flexibilities and Reprogramming
Singapore	• Departments are assigned a funding cap as a percentage of GDP, with exact budgets not made publicly available—MINDEF ceilings for each fiscal year are classified, but government has publicly committed to a goal of 3–4% of GDP. • Additional project funding can be obtained through a centralized Reinvestment Fund, which is funded through minor spending cuts, that allows reallocation of funds after a competitive bidding process among ministries, with the Ministry of Finance awarding funds. • Annual supplementary budget requests
Sweden	• "Special" or "extra" budget bills that allow for additional funds in response to unanticipated needs (COVID-19 pandemic) or changes to the security environment • Reprioritization of funds through a SwAF annual balancing process • Flexibility for reprogramming of resources within expenditure areas; parliamentary approval required for reallocation of funds between expenditure areas • Multiyear financial commitments with parliamentary approval

TABLE 4.10

Execution: U.S. and Comparative Nation Assessment Authorities

Country	Key Stakeholders in Execution Assessment
United States	• Under Secretary of Defense (Comptroller) • DoD component comptrollers and financial managers • Department of the Treasury • Government Accountability Office • OMB • Defense Finance and Accounting Service
China	• Military Expenditure Performance Management system; guideline-driven performance evaluations of military projects • Ministry of Finance Military Accounting System; evaluation using indicators, such as asset-liability ratios
Russia	• MoD • Federal Agency for State Property Management • Accounts Chamber
Australia	• National Audit Office • Finance regulations within Department of Defence and the public service • Defence Finance Policy Framework • Annual Performance Statement; submitted in October of the year following defense appropriation by the prime minister and cabinet • Portfolio Additional Estimates Statement; reflects budget appropriations and changes between budgets
Canada	• Auditor General • Parliamentary Budget Office • DND internal Review Services division
UK	• National Audit Office • Comptroller • Auditor General • HM Treasury (approval required for any MoD expenditure above £600 million, monthly and annual reporting from MoD on actual and forecasted spending, etc.) • House of Commons Public Accounts Committee

Table 4.10—Continued

Country	Key Stakeholders in Execution Assessment
France	• Court of Auditors • Defense Commission of the National Assembly • "Settlement law" at the end of a fiscal year to close accounts reports on past performance by mission, program, and operation • DGA internal control process for budget monitoring and tracking of armaments projects
Germany	• Budget Committee and Defense Committee of the Bundestag • "Mirror units" of each department in the BMF to track and monitor spending • Federal Court of Audit
Japan	• Board of Audit of Japan (independent entity) • Internal reviews by ministries
Singapore	• Internal (MINDEF's Internal Audit Department) and external (Auditor-General's Office Singapore) audits of MINDEF • Parliamentary oversight through the Estimates Committee, the Public Accounts Committee, and the Parliamentary Committee on Defence and Foreign Affairs • Corrupt Practices Investigation Bureau
Sweden	• SwAF annual evaluation report • National Audit Office • Fiscal Policy Council • National Institute for Economic Research • National Financial Management Authority • National Debt Office

Summary of Budgetary Flexibilities of DoD and Comparative U.S. Federal Agencies

In Tables 4.11 through 4.14, we summarize the budgetary flexibilities of the assessed non-DoD U.S. federal agencies, compared with DoD budgetary flexibilities. As an introduction, Table 4.11 specifies each agency's planning and budget system. Table 4.12 summarizes the funding categories and funding availability within each system. Table 4.13 compares the different types of carryover funds and restrictions during continuing resolutions. Table 4.14 focuses on the different kinds of reprogramming, transfers, and supplemental funding available within each system.[2]

---

[2] Information in these tables is derived from multiple sources cited in Volumes 3 and 6. For full bibliographic details, see McKernan, Young, Consaul, et al. (2024) and Young, McKernan, Consaul, et al. (2024).

TABLE 4.11

Planning and Budget Systems of DoD and Comparative U.S. Agencies

Agency	Planning and Budget System
DoD	Planning, Programming, Budgeting, and Execution (PPBE) System
DHS	Future Years Homeland Security Program (FYHSP)
HHS	No direct analog at departmental level; operating divisions (OPDIVs) have individual approaches to annual budget planning and formulation
NASA	PPBE System
ODNI	Intelligence Planning, Programming, Budgeting, and Evaluation (IPPBE) System
VA	No direct analog at departmental level; ad hoc process relying on governance boards and internal reviews that focuses on budgeting and execution—strategic planning is not well aligned with related processes
NNSA	Planning, Programming, Budgeting, and Evaluation (PPBE) process

NOTE: DHS = U.S. Department of Homeland Security; HHS = U.S. Department of Health and Human Services; NASA = National Aeronautics and Space Administration; ODNI = Office of the Director of National Intelligence.

TABLE 4.12

Funding Categories and Funding Availability for DoD and Comparative U.S. Agencies

Agency	Funding Categories	Funding Availability
DoD	• Discretionary budget includes Military Personnel (MILPERS), Operations and Maintenance (O&M), Procurement, RDT&E, and Construction (Military Construction, Family Housing, and Base Realignment and Closure Program) account categories	• Varies by account type; multiyear or no-year appropriations for limited programs as authorized by Congress
DHS	• Discretionary budget includes component-level accounts organized by four common categories • Mandatory funding for some functions, such as Coast Guard benefits • Some activities funded through discretionary fees and collections	• Varies by account type; multiyear or no-year appropriations for certain programs as authorized
HHS	• Discretionary budget organized under 12 OPDIVs • Mandatory funding is ~90% of budget • Some activities funded through discretionary fees	• One-year appropriations for most of discretionary operational budget; multiyear and no-year appropriations for certain programs
NASA	• Discretionary budget with output-oriented appropriations allocated at program level	• Six-year appropriations, construction • Two-year appropriations (except Office of Inspector General and Construction and Environmental Compliance and Restoration), all other account types
ODNI	• Discretionary budget for National Intelligence Program (NIP) activities managed by ODNI • Discretionary budget for Military Intelligence Program (MIP) activities managed through DoD	• Varies by account type; one-year appropriations for ODNI operations

Table 4.12—Continued

Agency	Funding Categories	Funding Availability
VA	• Budget organized by function; mix of mandatory and discretionary funding • Mandatory funding is ~60% of budget and includes veterans' disability compensation, pensions, life insurance, living allowances, and burial benefits • Discretionary funding includes ongoing medical care programs and operating activities (construction, electronic health record modernization, information technology [IT], and other operating expenses)	• Varies by function; discretionary budget includes mix of one-year, multiyear, and no-year appropriations • Discretionary and mandatory accounts receive advance appropriations for certain veterans' medical care and benefits programs, available one year after appropriation
NNSA	• Discretionary budget includes Weapons Activities, Defense Nuclear Nonproliferation, Naval Reactors, and Federal Salaries and Expenses account categories • No specific types of funding appropriations or *colors of money* allows the movement of funds within each program or project under the account categories without reprogramming	• No-year appropriations for majority of operational budget

TABLE 4.13

Carryover Funds and Restrictions for DoD and Comparative U.S. Agencies

Agency	Carryover Funds	Restrictions During Continuing Resolutions
DoD	• Limited carryover authority in accordance with OMB Circular A-11	• Various; no new programs, increases in production rates, etc.
DHS	• Authority to carry over one-year operations and support (O&S) funding into the next fiscal year; can expend up to 50% of prior-year lapsed balance	• Various; no new programs, new hiring, or new contract awards for discretionary programs
HHS	• Limited carryover authority in accordance with OMB Circular A-11	• Various; new contract awards and grants have been suspended for discretionary programs.
NASA	• Limited carryover authority in accordance with OMB Circular A-11	• Minimal; two-year appropriations and 90–95% obligation goal for first year of availability allow forward funding of contracts.
ODNI	• Limited carryover authority in accordance with OMB Circular A-11	• Restrictions on ODNI/NIP operations are unclear; MIP operations are subject to restrictions on DoD activities during continuing resolutions.
VA	• Authority to carry forward funding related to medical care programs, subject to a ceiling; additional percentage-based carryover authority threshold for one-year appropriations	• Varies by function; minimal to no impact on veterans' medical care and benefit programs receiving advance appropriations, as well as on accounts with multiyear and no-year funding • Discretionary programs funded through one-year accounts are subject to prior–fiscal year funding levels.
NNSA	• No-year appropriations for operational budget allows the carryover of unobligated funds from year to year.	• Minimal; carryover of prior-year balances allows continued, unrestricted operations.

TABLE 4.14

Reprogramming, Transfers, and Supplements for DoD and Comparative U.S. Agencies

Agency	Reprogramming	Transfers	Supplemental Funding
DoD	• As authorized; four defined categories of reprogramming actions • Prior-approval reprogramming actions—increasing procurement quantity of a major end item, establishing a new program, etc.—require approval from congressional defense committees	• As authorized; general and special transfer authorities, typically provided in defense authorization and appropriations acts	• Frequent; linked to emerging operational and national security needs
DHS	• As authorized; request to Congress must be made before June 30 if additional support for emerging needs or crises exceeds 10% of original appropriated funding • Restrictions (creation of program, augmentation of funding in excess of $5M or 10%, reduction of funding by ≥10%, etc.) absent notification	• As authorized; up to 5% of current fiscal-year appropriations may be transferred if appropriations committees are notified at least 30 days in advance; transfer may not represent >10% increase to an individual program except as otherwise specified	• Frequent; linked to Disaster Relief Fund for domestic disaster and emergency response and recovery
HHS	• As authorized; no notification below threshold of lesser of $1M or 10% of an account; notification of reprogramming actions above this threshold required • Notification required above threshold of $500K if reprogramming decreases appropriated funding by >10% or substantially affects program personnel or operations	• As authorized; Secretary's One-Percent Transfer General Provision allows transfer of up to 1% from any account into another account, not to exceed up to 3% of funds previously in account, maximum transfer amount of ~$900M	• Frequent; linked to public health crises, hurricane relief, and refugee resettlement support
NASA	• As authorized; reprogramming documents must be submitted if a budget account changes by $500K • Within the Exploration Systems and Space Operations account, no more than 10% of funds for Explorations Systems may be reprogrammed for Space Operations and vice versa	• As authorized; transfers for select purposes authorized by 51 U.S.C. § 20143	• Rare

Table 4.14—Continued

Agency	Reprogramming	Transfers	Supplemental Funding
ODNI	• As authorized; Director of National Intelligence (DNI) may reprogram funds within the NIP with the approval of the OMB Director and in consultation with affected agencies • Notification to Congress within 30 days for reprogramming actions >$10M or 5% when funds transferred in or out of NIP or between appropriation accounts • Notification to Congress of reprogramming actions prior to June 30	• As authorized; DNI may transfer funds within NIP with the approval of the OMB Director and in consultation with affected agencies	• Detailed funding profiles for NIP and MIP are not publicly available.
VA	• As authorized; annual appropriations legislation typically authorizes reprogramming actions for certain accounts, subject to limitations ($7M or 25% of an account for construction programs; $1M for IT programs) • Notification to Congress required for above-threshold reprogramming actions and certain categories of reprogramming actions	• As authorized; Recurring Expenses Transformational Fund allows reallocation of expired, unobligated funds to an account for department-wide purposes, such as Veterans Health Administration facility infrastructure improvements and IT modernization	• Rare; post extension of authority to request advance appropriations for veterans' medical care and benefits programs
NNSA	• As authorized; annual appropriations legislation typically authorizes internal reprogramming actions, subject to limitations ($5M or 10% of any annual funding level) • Notification to Congress and 30-day waiting period required for above-threshold reprogramming actions, which must be cleared through NNSA, DOE, and OMB • Reprogramming authorities do not allow the creation, initiation, or elimination of a program, project, or activity. • Reprogramming authorities cannot be used to increase funds or personnel for any program, project, or activity for which Congress has previously denied funds.	• As authorized by 50 U.S.C. § 2745; allows transfer of up to 5% of previously authorized funds between DOE account categories, subject to certain limitations and congressional notification	• Rare; no-year appropriations allows funding of unanticipated needs using prior-year balances

Abbreviations

CAPE	Office of Cost Assessment and Program Evaluation
CEPE	Office of Cost Estimating and Program Evaluation
COVID-19	coronavirus disease 2019
DHS	U.S. Department of Homeland Security
DoD	U.S. Department of Defense
FY	fiscal year
GDP	gross domestic product
HHS	U.S. Department of Health and Human Services
IT	information technology
NASA	National Aeronautics and Space Administration
NATO	North Atlantic Treaty Organization
NNSA	National Nuclear Security Administration
ODNI	Office of the Director of National Intelligence
PPBE	Planning, Programming, Budgeting, and Evaluation (NNSA)
PPBE	Planning, Programming, Budgeting, and Execution
RDT&E	research, development, test, and evaluation
UK	United Kingdom
VA	U.S. Department of Veterans Affairs

References

Commission on Planning, Programming, Budgeting, and Execution (PPBE) Reform, *Interim Report*, U.S. Senate, August 2023.

Greenwalt, William, and Dan Patt, *Competing in Time: Ensuring Capability Advantage and Mission Success Through Adaptable Resource Allocation*, Hudson Institute, February 2021.

McGarry, Brendan W., *DOD Planning, Programming, Budgeting, and Execution (PPBE): Overview and Selected Issues for Congress*, Congressional Research Service, R47178, July 11, 2022.

McKernan, Megan, Stephanie Young, Ryan Consaul, Michael Simpson, Sarah W. Denton, Anthony Vassalo, William Shelton, Devon Hill, Raphael S. Cohen, John P. Godges, Heidi Peters, and Lauren Skrabala, *Planning, Programming, Budgeting, and Execution in Comparative Organizations:* Vol. 3, *Case Studies of Selected Non-DoD Federal Agencies*, RAND Corporation, RR-A2195-3, 2024. As of January 23, 2024:
https://www.rand.org/pubs/research_reports/RRA2195-3.html

McKernan, Megan, Stephanie Young, Andrew Dowse, James Black, Devon Hill, Benjamin J. Sacks, Austin Wyatt, Nicolas Jouan, Yuliya Shokh, Jade Yeung, Raphael S. Cohen, John P. Godges, Heidi Peters, and Lauren Skrabala, *Planning, Programming, Budgeting, and Execution in Comparative Organizations:* Vol. 2, *Case Studies of Selected Allied and Partner Nations*, RAND Corporation, RR-A2195-2, 2024. As of January 23, 2024:
https://www.rand.org/pubs/research_reports/RRA2195-2.html

McKernan, Megan, Stephanie Young, Timothy R. Heath, Dara Massicot, Andrew Dowse, Devon Hill, James Black, Ryan Consaul, Michael Simpson, Sarah W. Denton, Anthony Vassalo, Ivana Ke, Mark Stalczynski, Benjamin J. Sacks, Austin Wyatt, Jade Yeung, Nicolas Jouan, Yuliya Shokh, William Shelton, Raphael S. Cohen, John P. Godges, Heidi Peters, and Lauren Skrabala, *Planning, Programming, Budgeting, and Execution in Comparative Organizations:* Vol. 4, *Executive Summary*, RAND Corporation, RR-A2195-4, 2024. As of January 23, 2024:
https://www.rand.org/pubs/research_reports/RRA2195-4.html

McKernan, Megan, Stephanie Young, Timothy R. Heath, Dara Massicot, Mark Stalczynski, Ivana Ke, Raphael S. Cohen, John P. Godges, Heidi Peters, and Lauren Skrabala, *Planning, Programming, Budgeting, and Execution in Comparative Organizations:* Vol. 1, *Case Studies of China and Russia*, RAND Corporation, RR-A2195-1, 2024. As of January 23, 2024:
https://www.rand.org/pubs/research_reports/RRA2195-1.html

Public Law 117-81, National Defense Authorization Act for Fiscal Year 2022, December 27, 2021.

Section 809 Panel, *Report of the Advisory Panel on Streamlining and Codifying Acquisition Regulations*, Vol. 2 of 3, June 2018.

U.S. Government, "Budget FY 1996—Analytical Perspectives, Budget of the United States Government, Fiscal Year 1996," February 1, 1995.

Young, Stephanie, Megan McKernan, Ryan Consaul, Laurinda L. Rohn, Frank G. Klotz, Michael Simpson, Sarah W. Denton, Yuliya Shokh, Madison Williams, Raphael S. Cohen, John P. Godges, Heidi Peters, and Lauren Skrabala, *Planning, Programming, Budgeting, and Execution in Comparative Organizations:* Vol. 6, *Additional Case Studies of Selected Non-DoD Federal Agencies*, RAND Corporation, RR-A2195-6, 2024. As of April 25, 2024:
https://www.rand.org/pubs/research_reports/RRA2195-6.html

Young, Stephanie, Megan McKernan, Andrew Dowse, Nicolas Jouan, Theodora Ogden, Austin Wyatt, Mattias Eken, Linda Slapakova, Naoko Aoki, Clara Le Gargasson, Charlotte Kleberg, Maxime Sommerfeld Antoniou, Phoebe Felicia Pham, Jade Yeung, Turner Ruggi, Erik Silfversten, James Black, Raphael S. Cohen, John P. Godges, Heidi Peters, and Lauren Skrabala, *Planning, Programming, Budgeting, and Execution in Comparative Organizations:* Vol. 5, *Additional Case Studies of Selected Allied and Partner Nations*, RAND Corporation, RR-A2195-5, 2024. As of April 25, 2024:
https://www.rand.org/pubs/research_reports/RRA2195-5.html